Dedicated to my loving, supportive family.

To my mother who taught me to sew a seam.
To my father who taught me to sow a life.
To my daughters, Sarah and Noelle, who taught me so much about living.
And to my husband, Allen, who taught me so, so, so much about dreams.

I am also grateful to the many teachers, administrators, parents, librarians, park folks, and fellow performers who have loved this project into existence. I appreciate your encouragement.

Special thanks to Linda Batley of Quilter's Quest, Door County, for loaning me her sewing machine and also introducing me to the concept of paper piecing.

I am deeply indebted to the generations of quilters past and the current quilt artists whose work is both marvelous and an inspiration. I am most in awe of the body of work created by Aminah Brenda Lynn Robinson. You are a blessing, and I am better for having known you.

DJC

Quilt Art and Illustrations Copyright © 2004 Debbie Clement
Text Copyright © 1997 Debbie Clement
From *Debbie's Ditties for Little Kiddies*
Recording produced @ Amerisound Studio © 1997

Arrangement by Tom Martin
Vocals by Debbie Clement & Dan Green
Engineered by Dan Green
Guitar by Larry Cook

Book layout and graphic design by Lynn Wheeler
Information Design, Worthington, Ohio

Library of Congress Cataloging-in-Publication Data
Clement, Debbie.
    You're Wonderful/by Debbie Clement
    Artwork/by Debbie Clement
Summary: A song of self-esteem and hope sung between adult and child, celebrated through the use of colorful quilted illustrations, expanded by sign language.

Published by Rainbows Within Reach
www.rainbowswithinreach.com
Columbus, Ohio

Distributed by Express Fulfillment
1000 F Taylor Station Road
Columbus, OH 43230
1 (866) 866-7515 Toll Free

Additional Recordings by Debbie Clement
    Debbie's Ditties 2 Much Fun
    Debbie's Ditties 3 At the Library
    Debbie's Ditties 4 Come Dance S'More

ISBN 0-9705987-4-2

You're Wonderful

by Debbie Clement

··· Published by Rainbows Within Reach ···

"I think you're wonderful.

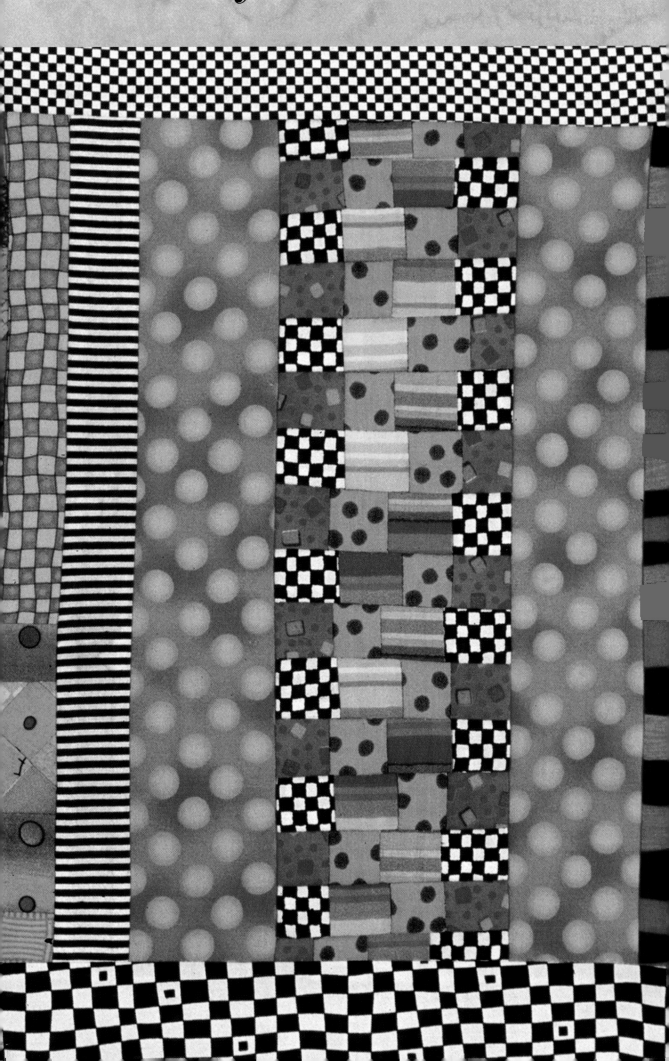

and filled with curiosity and dreams."

"You think I'm wonderful?

You think I'm marvelous?"

"You think I'm beautiful, and magical,

and filled with curiosity and dreams?"

"You're right I'm wonderful.

You're right I'm marvelous."

"You're right I'm beautiful, and magical,

and filled with curiosity and dreams."

"I think you're wonderful.

I think you're marvelous."

"I think you're beautiful, and magical,

and filled with curiosity and dreams."

"You're right I'm wonderful.

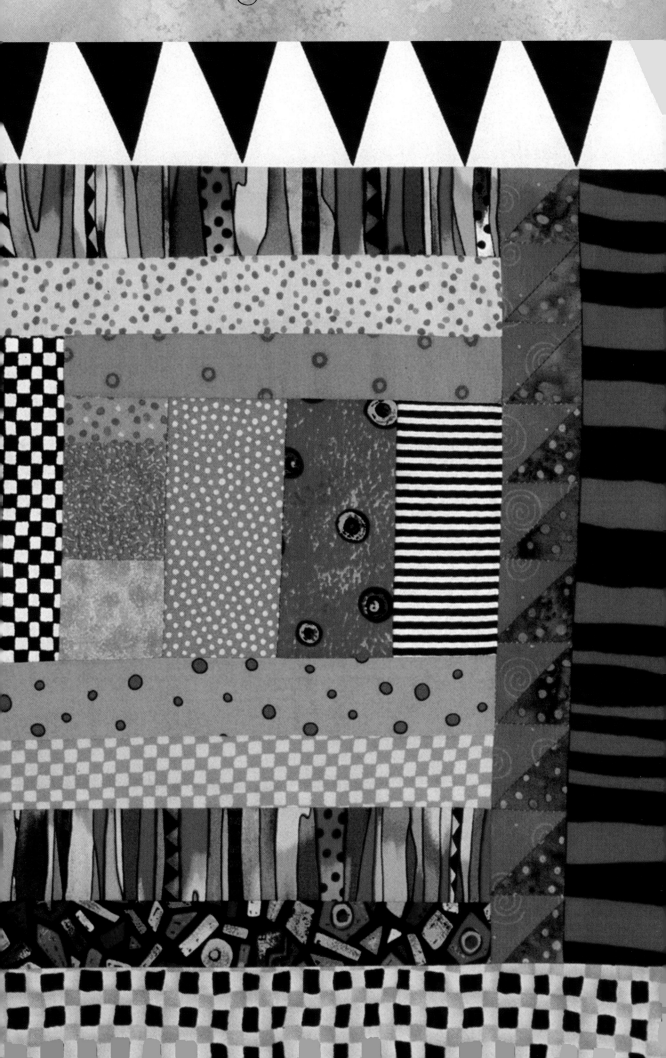

and filled with curiosity and dreams."

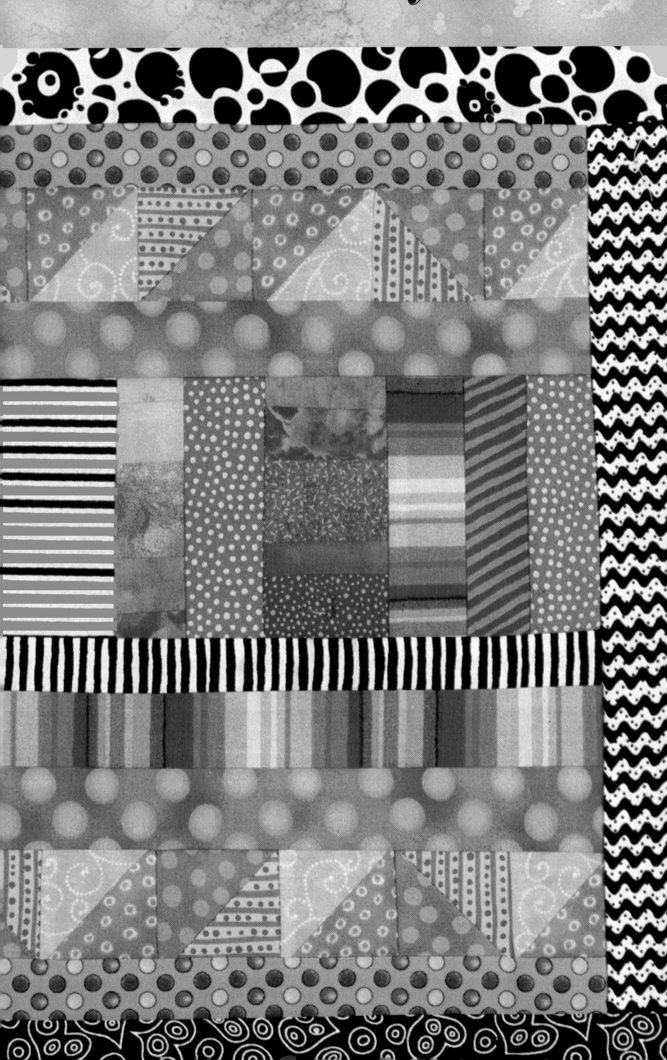

"That means we're wonderful.

...and filled with curiosity...

...and dreams!!"

...filled with curiosity...

wonderful...

marvelous...

beautiful...

magical...

SIGN LANGUAGE

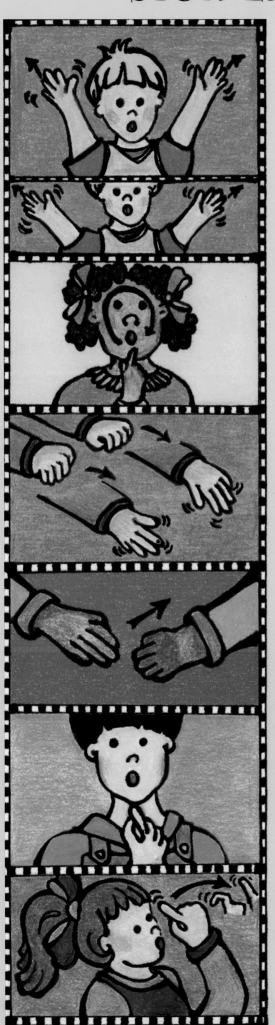

Wonderful

Move the flat open hands (palms out, fingers up) forward in front of each side of the head.

(a gesture of awe & wonder)

Marvelous

Repeat sign for 'wonderful'.

Beautiful

Place the fingertips of the right hand @ the chin & make a large circular movement around face.

(hand encircles a beautiful face)

Magical

Hold both closed hands in front of body.... open fingers with a quick forward movement.

(the hands seem to cast a spell)

Filled

Move the right palm across the top of the closed left hand.

(indicates container full, level off to brim)

Curiosity

Pinch neck slightly with right hand & wiggle.

(Adam's apple was eaten out of curiosity)

Dreams

Touch forehead with right index finger, move finger away, bending & unbending.

(imagination ventures out from mind)

- wonderful
- marvelous
- beautiful
- magical
- curiosity
- dreams

♪ The Story of the Song ♪

The words we use make a deep impact. Their choice deserves care and attention. The use of positive affirmations for our children and our students is vital to their well being.

I wrote this song during the most challenging time of my life. With husband Allen as pilot, we flew off over lake Michigan. Suddenly, the clouds 'literally' parted for me. Sun broke through. "This is wonderful."

Repeating that phrase I felt hope. I heard the voice of Mary Moyer, our theraplay therapist from the Childhood League Center, using affirmations for our children with special needs. She had us hold these little ones and say "I think you're wonderful."

I pondered what the child must have felt. "You think I'm wonderful?..... I can't pedal a tricycle, I just spilled paint." We continued with the affirmations in the hope of making a connection.

The song unfolded before the plane landed, scratched verses on a scrap of paper. I gave words and tune to Tom Martin who crafted the arrangement. Recording began at Amerisound, Dan Green as engineer. I realized I needed another 'voice' to represent the child and Dan left the console and sang. Larry Cook added the guitar tracks. "Debbie's Ditties for Little Kiddies" was born. The year was 1997.

Amazing feedback. Adults cried as I taught the song at conferences. People shared stories of using it: preschool graduation, Mother's Day tea, teenage mommy class, on a hospital ward, in time of family distress. I realized the need for words of hope. I was taught sign language to support the song by librarian, Annette Sheldon. I taught it at the Marysville Women's Prison to visiting children of inmates.

My 'dream' had always been to create a book. Initially I thought I'd illustrate with children's faces. I realized the limitations in selecting any specific children as models. On a return flight to Door County I attended a show by quilt artist Sue Benner and painter Judi Ekholm. The color was powerful. I recalled the Columbus Museum of Art's retrospective of Aminah Robinson. (I had returned many times to drink in her unique vision.) And the seeds sown began to sprout. Could I create quilts as illustrations? Graphic. Bold. Open ended.

As with all my projects I realized this would be a walk of faith. I had no idea how it could work. I went to the library and checked out as many books on quilting as I could carry. I studied the work of Sassaman, Crow, Porcella, Moran, Wells, and began. I cut. I pieced.

The kitchen was awash with fabric. A small 'quiltlet' emerged, my ode to 'empty nesting' as our girls, Sarah and Noelle, had each recently departed for their own new lives as adults.

I sewed before my daily 'artist-in-the-school' visits. I pieced in the midst of holidays (the Christmas tree never got decorated, laundry mounted.) The 'quiltlets' grew in number. I sent publishing proposals and received rejection letters. Friends Sarah Schneider and mentor Mimi Chenfeld encouraged. I anxiously tip-toed into new Quilt Trends, and shared the work with owners Dave and Sue Sandritter --- they cheered!

Then serendipity. I shared the 'quiltlets-in-process' during a keynote presentation for the Columbus Assoc for the Education of Young Children. Fran Conway, of 'Experiences' suggested I create a poster. I enlisted the skills of Lynn Wheeler. She digitally quilted the quilts and the poster was born. AMEN! Then Lynn continued to refine and direct me through the process of crafting the book. If you are holding it in your hands, my dream has come true. HALLELUJAH! It takes a village.

Thank you family, friends, and angels for your support.... mom, dad, Allen, kids, I love you.

Debbie Clement July 2004

You were wonderfully made, now go make something wonderful.

You're Wonderful

D. Clement/ Arr. by T. Martin

Verse 3

You're right I'm wonderful.
You're right I'm marvelous.
You're right I'm beautiful, and magical,
and filled with curiosity and dreams.

Verse 4

I think you're wonderful.
I think you're marvelous.
I think you're beautiful, and magical,
and filled with curiosity and dreams.

Verse 5

You're right I'm wonderful.
You're right I'm marvelous.
You're right I'm beautiful, and magical,
and filled with curiosity and dreams.

Verse 6

That means we're wonderful.
That means we're marvelous.
That means we're beautiful, and magical,
and filled with curiosity and dreams!!

Coda

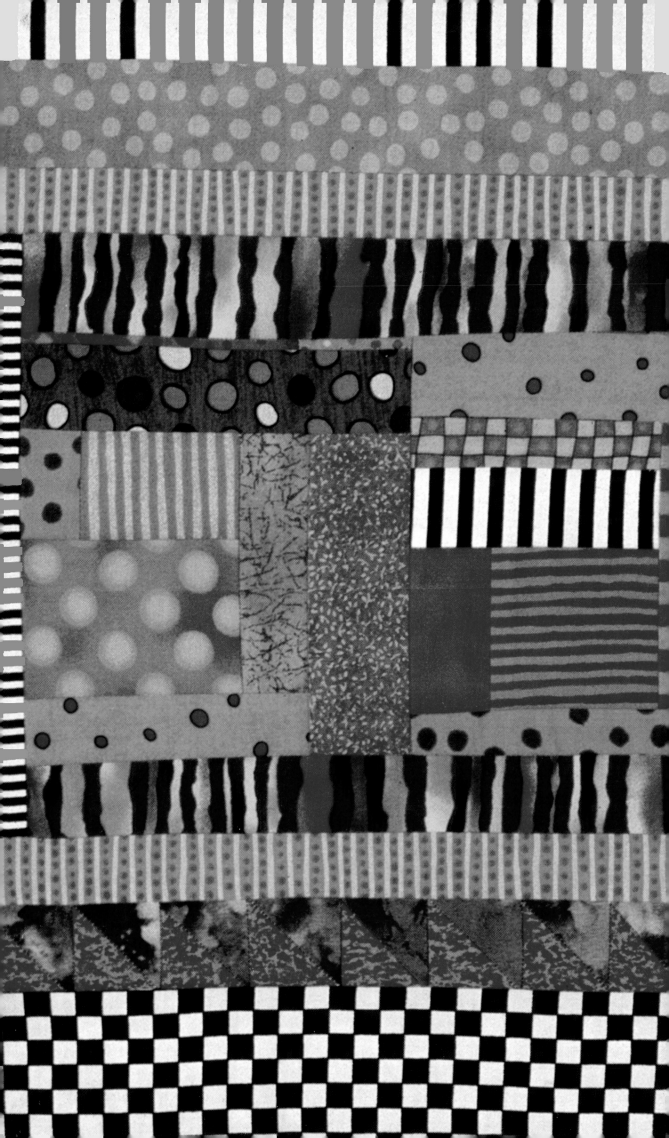